AF255904

'Tis not in mortals to command success, but we will do more—deserve it.[1]

Evening Express. "Public Amusements." January 31, 1898.

ERIK ÅBERG

CLEVERER THAN GOD

Echoes and Excerpts from the Life of Paul Cinquevalli

MODERN VAUDEVILLE PRESS

2023

The world's a theatre; the Earth a stage

Sylvius. "THE THEATRE." *The Dominion*, August 17, 1912.

ISBN: 978-1-958604-11-3
ISSN: 2002-603X
Publication Series: X Position no. 26.
Library of Congress: 2023924529
www.erikaberg.com
www.modernvaudevillepress.com
www.uniarts.se

For my mother Eva,
who always asks about Paul.

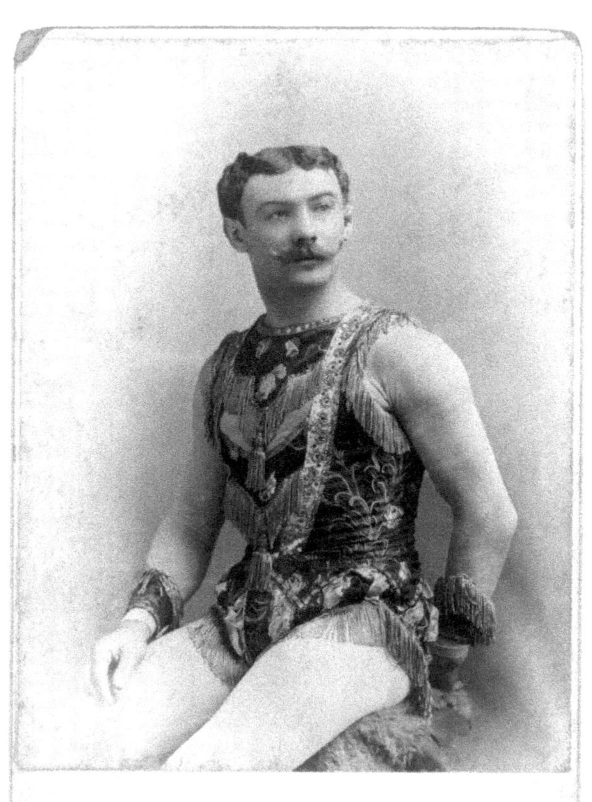

Warwick Brookes
350 OXFORD ROAD
MANCHESTER.

A juggler, I think, like a poet,
must be born, not made.

The Daily Independent: Helena. "THE JUGGLER BORN."

December 30, 1894.

CONTENTS

PROLOGUE

~

The dinner commenced as all respectable dinners do, with soup. When this was brought on the host took up the dish, threw it into the air, caught it on his forefinger, and spun it round and round over the table. This feat almost took away the breath of several of his guests, and one or two ladies removed their chairs to a safe distance. Then the host turned round to them and smiled. "It's only cooling," he observed calmly.

The Southern Echo. "A MODERN WIZARD."
February 22, 1898.

Whenever Paul Cinquevalli was asked about his life, an amusing anecdote invariably made its entrance. For him, questions served merely as openings for the creation of yet another bit of entertainment, and it remains uncertain if he ever harbored a desire for his true story to be etched in history. No memoir bears his name, and despite forging friendships with several esteemed authors who held him in high regard, no scribe endeavored to chronicle his existence.[2] [3]

What remains are fragments, often dictated by Cinquevalli himself, showcasing his virtuosity as a masterful storyteller. He skillfully wove his artistry into the very fabric of his life's tales, transcending the confines of just stage performance. Pinpointing the precise boundary between where his narrative concludes and authentic reality begins, proves an insurmountable challenge. In the present day, the memory of Paul Cinquevalli has all but faded into obscurity. However, if we were to glance at the press clippings from 1896, an entirely different narrative would surface:

> Every boy in New York knows him.
> Cinquevalli is as popular as Mark Twain.
>
> *Der Artist*, [Author's translation] February 2, 1902.

Numerous brief accounts exist regarding his illustrious personality, fame and accomplishments. Yet, the task of constructing a comprehensive portrait continues to pose its challenges. Who was this individual whom the author E.V. Lucas deemed to be "worth sitting through an hour of rubbish to witness five minutes of"?[4]

DECIPHERING THE PRONOUNCIATION OF "CINQUEVALLI"

_~_

"Chink," said Mr Cinquevalli; "Yes, you've got it right. I'm used to hearing my name pronounced all sorts of ways, but you've got the Chink right."

The _Daily Mail_. "AN ENGLISHMAN FROM CHOICE. CINQUEVALLI, THE JUGGLER, ON MANY THINGS." February 8, 1904.

In the early stages of his international career, Cinquevalli placed great emphasis on his presumed Italian heritage, even adopting the honorific "Signor"[5] [6] before his name in print. Drawing from the Italian word for "five" - "Cinque," and appending "Valli" to it, he arrived at "Chin-cooeh-valli," as close to Italian as one could reasonably expect from a Polish-German artist[7] [8] who had moved between St. Petersburg and Odessa,[9] lived on tour through Spain,[10] Austria,[11] Switzerland,[12] Denmark,[13] Sweden,[14] and France.[15]

However, as he gradually became more anglicized over the years, his own pronunciation inched closer to "Chinky-Walley".[16] The public, however, never reached a consensus on a definitive pronunciation, and throughout his career, several versions kept floating around.

I heard Cinquevalli called so many different ways I wouldn't begin to settle down on any.

Los Angeles Herald. "Horses With Great Names."
July 9, 1903.

The usual weird struggle with the pronunciation of a foreign name. Cinquevalli is variously called "Sinkovalli," "Sankevalli,"[17] "Kinkevalli," and "Chinkevalli." Last correct.

The Critic. "Various Views." June 3, 1899.

Jugglers come and jugglers go, but "Chink" (as he is called for short) not only seems inclined to go on for ever, but also to go on for ever improving.

The Referee. "The Big Star." January 6, 1901.

THE LITTLE FLYING DEVIL[18]

~

One of my names is Paul, but Cinquevalli I took from the first acrobat I was under.

The Australian Star. "STAGE CELEBRITIES."
June 27, 1899.

Emil Otto Paul Braun graced the world on the 30th of June, 1859, in the town of Lissa[19] in the Kingdom of Prussia.[20] Nevertheless, it was in the vibrant streets of Berlin where he grew into his own.[21] Throughout his childhood he had no relation to the name Cinquevalli.

After winning several prizes at a gymnastics competition by the age of twelve,[22] his family was invited to the theatre by a spectator from the competition that had been very impressed by Paul's extraordinary abilities. Little did they know that this spectator was none other than Leopold Cinquevalli, a seasoned trapeze artiste with his own troupe.[23] [24] As a reward for his winnings, Paul's father agreed to accompany him to the theater that very evening. It was an entirely novel experience for him, and he was captivated by the assortment of acts and the prowess of the artistes. Suddenly, Leopold appeared on stage and gave a truly spectacular performance. Young Paul, who had seen nothing like it previously, was completely enthralled.

> I know I must become a gymnast; it was fate.
>
> *The Weekly Dispatch.* "PAUL CINQUEVALLI TELLS HOW HE BECAME THE TRICKIEST MAN ON EARTH." May 13, 1900.

Following the conclusion of the spectacle, Leopold made his way back to the Braun family, and disclosed his actual intention with the invitation. He asked if Paul wanted to join the troupe.

> My father, who wished me to enter the priesthood, was righteously horrified. He bade the distinguished stranger a cold "Good night" and hurried me out of the presence of such temptation.
>
> *The Kansas City Star.* "THE ART OF THE JUGGLER." October 6, 1901.

But the magnetism of adventure had already captured Paul with its inescapable attraction. Surrendering to its call, in secret from his parents, he arranged for his departure with his enticer whose name he also adopted. It was now, that he became Paul Cinquevalli. Initially, it served as a means to navigate border inspections, later as a member of the troupe, and eventually as a solo performer, cementing itself as his artistic *Nom de guerre.*

> The result was inevitable. A week later I had run away from home, and with my new acquaintance, whose name was Cinquevalli, was en route for Odessa. On reaching there I at once wrote home, and shortly after received a letter from my father giving me two months to return, or, failing to do so, to consider the family circle complete without me. I was only a boy of twelve and my new life fascinated me. I did not return.

> The next two years passed very quickly. According to all well regulated story-books, I should have bitterly repented my decision and returned home, like the Prodigal Son, but things in real life don't always follow the rules laid out in books.

> *The Examiner.* "HAS HE A SIXTH SENSE?"
> January 4, 1891.

He was obliged to obtain a social passport, and being unable to do that of himself, he was aided by an old acrobat, who added to his own passport, which was issued to "Leopold Cinquevalli," the words "and son," so from that day he has adopted the name under which he goes but which was not the one he bore at his christening.

The Detroit Free Press. "HOW TO BECOME AN EXPERT JUGGLER." February 19, 1902.

At the age of thirteen he ran away from home and joined a noted performer at Odessa. Under his guidance Cinquevalli's fame as an aerial performer was soon noised abroad, and he was nicknamed the Little Flying Devil.

The Referee. "People Prominent." June 28, 1899.

The love for your parents is not strong enough when destiny is calling.

Ziethen, Karl-Heinz. 4,000 Years of Juggling. Vol. 1. 2 vols. Sainte-Geneviève, Editions Michel Poignant, 1981.

THE FEELING OF BONES, BREAKING

I ran away, and at first was cursed, but I made my name,
and that altered matters.

The Australian Star. "STAGE CELEBRITIES."
June 27, 1899.

Paul Braun, now known as Paul Cinquevalli, and affectionately hailed as the "Little Flying Devil," immersed himself in the thrilling world of aerial acrobatics and the joys that life as a performer had to offer. But the wonders of his newfound existence would prove to be short-lived.

They love to see a performance that has a spice of danger in it, and the aerial feats that Cinquevalli[25] and I performed, such as long leaps, high-up-in-the-air and dizzy tumblings and turning on lofty trapezes and rings with no safety-net below us, caught their fancy at once.

They nicknamed me the "Little Devil" and applauded me to my heart's content.

After performing in all of the principal cities in Russia we at length returned to Germany and played in nearly all of the larger cities there. At last we reached Berlin.

During these two years I had not written or received a word from my father. We were both too proud. With mother, however, it is very different, and I had no sooner set foot in my native town than she was there to meet me. That night, by request, our company gave a performance before the Emperor, and the next morning's papers were full of splendid "notices." I met my father face to face in one of the large cafés in Berlin and a minute later we were seated at a table. Friends once more. The past forgotten and forgiven. After touring through other parts of Europe I returned to Russia, and there the "smash" occurred. I was doing a long leap from one swinging trapeze to another. As usual, there was no net below. The attendant whose duty it was to wipe carefully from the bars of the trapeze the moisture that collects upon them in wet weather, drank [too] much vodka one evening, climbed up on the platform, wiped that bar, climbed down, drank some more, and forgot to wipe the other. When my turn came I climbed to my dizzy perch, grasped the bar, the dry one, unfortunately, and swung off. I remember sweeping through the air like a huge hawk, my eyes fixed on the other trapeze that swung to meet me. I let go, turned a somersault and seized the second trapeze. It slid through my fingers as if it had been greased. I heard a quick gasp of horror from the people below, and came to several days later in the hospital with more broken bones than I care to remember, and there I remained just eight months.

The Examiner. "HAS HE A SIXTH SENSE?"
January 4, 1891.

Throughout the course of Cinquevalli's illustrious career, a multitude of renditions of "the smash" story would emerge. Evidently, it stood as one of his most cherished tales to recount—a riveting saga that included his daring escape from home, the disastrous accident with the greased trapeze bar, and the triumphant return as a juggler, in front of a huge audience.

I was told afterwards that I knocked the front teeth down the throat of a Corporal of Cossacks, but I don't remember much about what happened afterwards.

Gubbins, Nathaniel. "BRANDY AND SODA" *The Sporting Times*, July 11, 1896.

And so, my career as an acrobat was truly finished, but I still had a string to my bow.

The Mail. "THE KING OF JUGGLERS - An Hour With Paul Cinquevalli." February 18, 1905.

GRAVITY, MY FRIEND, MY ENEMY

The law of gravitation had downed me once more. When I began to get better and was able to sit up and move about a little I began to fight again, but not with my own body. I had all I wanted of that. So I began to throw balls up in the air and balance bottles and things, as I used to do when I was a boy. It was pretty hard work at first. You see, I only had one hand to work with, but I stuck to it. **It was war to the death between Old Gravity and Paul Cinquevalli.** Every day I could see some gain. I could get more balls up in the air at once and keep them there longer. Plates, bottles and umbrellas got over trying to fall off the top of my nose and balanced there as if they enjoyed it. Then my left arm began to take a hand in the game. It was dreadfully stiff at first, and I used to think that my right hand was ashamed of its clumsy partner. Hour after hour I would practice juggling and hour after hour I kept getting more expert.

There is not much more to tell. I have never done "aerial work," as we call it, since that smash. I have stuck to the juggling and I think I have my old opponent, the law of gravitation, pretty well under my thumb.

The Examiner. "HAS HE A SIXTH SENSE?"
January 4, 1891.

After some practice, he pieced together a juggling act, and convinces Ernest Rost, director of the St. Petersburg Zoological Garden[26] to let him perform in the same place where his career as an acrobat had met an untimely conclusion.

Dressed in an Albert coat, I stepped on the very same stage on which I had fallen nearly twelve months before, but instead of the wild bursts of applause that usually greeted me, there was nothing but a strange stillness, which seemed to chill me to my very half-healed bones. Then it seemed as if the platform was commencing to sink down into the earth, and the sea of faces began to disappear as if enveloped by some haze. In another second the band struck the first note of the Russian Thanksgiving Hymn, and 14,000 people dropped on their knees, crossed themselves, and thanked the Almighty for my recovery.

The Weekly Dispatch. "PAUL CINQUEVALLI TELLS HOW HE BECAME THE TRICKIEST MAN ON EARTH." May 13, 1900.

The transformation from trapeze artist to juggler had now been completed. Cinquevalli's dedication to his craft was nothing short of fanatical, he must have spent countless hours devoted to practice each day. However, the mastery of juggling is an incremental process. The variations often require a combination of abilities that demands the juggler to develop into something like a hybrid between boxer and violin player. The astonishing feats of Cinquevalli required strength, agility, grace, explosiveness, and unwavering accuracy. Patience and perseverance[27 - 29] were indispensable ingredients in this endeavor, as the new path was far from a seamless journey, riddled with numerous obstacles along the way.

When business was not too good I wrestled.
That is how I got this thick ear.

The Daily Standard. "CINQUEVALLI RETIRES."
November 21, 1914, Second edition.

In 1881, Cinquevalli finally settles in the vibrant city of Paris,[30] and stays for three years. One day, fate intervenes, and a member of the Rothschild family attends his performance,[31] leading to a pivotal recommendation to the renowned London agent S.A. Parravicini. This fortunate encounter secures Cinquevalli a coveted spot in the Christmas performances at the Covent Garden Circus, with a grand premiere scheduled for Boxing Day in 1885.[32]

> But, my dear friends, have you seen that juggler Cinquevalli? He is a veritable wonder. I suppose he is paid a tremendous salary ; but whatever the figure may be, he is worth it. Such combination of strength, judgement, and dexterity I have never seen.

> *The Entr'acte*. "Merry-go-Round." January 16, 1886. p. 4.

The triumph at Covent Garden Circus was instantaneous.[33] London was the spark that set Cinquevalli's trajectory off like a comet. News of his astonishing performance quickly reaches the ears of the Prince of Wales, who, accompanied by his entire family, shows up a few days after the premiere.[34] Prince Edward is enraptured and calls Cinquevalli over to his box for a chat.[35] [36] The conversation ends with an invitation to perform at the Marlborough house, exclusively for the

Prince and his esteemed circle of friends. Naturally, the press catches wind of this sensational event,[37-39] and within a year, Cinquevalli becomes a household name across the United Kingdom. Interviews and pictures of him appear in the newspapers,[40-45] and he goes on to star in pantomimes alongside singers and actors.[46] Regular tours take him to the United States,[47-53] Australia,[54-57] and South Africa.[58 59] Juggling, once a mere curiosity,[60] becomes an established phenomenon in the world,[61] and an army of imitators emerge in the wake of Cinquevalli's meteoric rise.[62 63]

> Oh, yes, I have been over a good part of the world. My time is divided between New York, London, and Paris, which gives just change enough to suit me.
>
> *The New York Dramatic Mirror.* "VAUDEVILLE STAGE. THE KING OF JUGGLERS." January 25, 1896.

TO CATCH, OR TO DIE

A 48-lb. cannon-ball is hoisted 40ft. It rests on a collapsible shelf at that height, and the shelf is controlled by a spring connected with a bolt. Immediately beneath the ball is placed a strong table. The string is jerked, and down comes the cannon-ball, and smashes the table into firewood. Then Cinquevalli takes the place of the table, and the cannon-ball falls on his neck.

The Evening Journal. "THE PRINCE OF JUGGLERS. ARRIVAL OF M. PAUL CINQUEVALLI." April 24, 1899.

Prior to Cinquevalli's rise to fame, jugglers in Europe often used brass balls, knives, or objects of Asian origin[64][65] in their performances. Juggling itself carried an air of esotericism, leaving spectators uncertain about the type of ability that was required to execute such acts. Was it magic? Nevertheless, Cinquevalli revolutionized the art by making it relatable, employing everyday objects with complete transparency and openly asserting that ceaseless practice served as the bedrock of his abilities.

Then the idea came to me. Why should juggling always be done with shining brass balls? Why not use the things of ordinary life? I worked out the idea, and I soon had an 'act' ready. That brought about a revolution in juggling tricks.

The Daily Mail. "AN ENGLISHMAN FROM CHOICE. CINQUEVALLI, THE JUGGLER, ON MANY THINGS." February 8, 1904.

I make it a rule always to use for my tricks the ordinary articles of everyday life. It is more interesting to the public than elaborate apparatus. They can go home and try for themselves.

The Pall Mall Gazette. "A GREAT JUGGLER ON JUGGLING. An Interview with M. Paul Cinquevalli." May 21, 1886.

It is precisely this mentality that guided Cinquevalli towards a preference for objects like cigars, hats, umbrellas, cups, and candles for his feats.[66]

As a finale, his attendant, who weighs 10st,[67] seated himself at a table, and Cinquevalli lifted the whole–man, chair, and table–above his head, after which he supported them in his mouth while he juggled with several balls. Such a feat has never before been seen here, and it not unnaturally sent the audience wild with enthusiasm.

The Referee. "People Prominent." June 28, 1899.

According to Cinquevalli himself, he dedicated 3 to 4 hours nearly every day of his life to practice,[68] and claimed to have invented more than 3000 feats.[69] [70] It was widely reported about the challenging journey behind executing and conquering a particular trick, like his famous egg catch:

> If you want to have your hair stand up in astonishment, you must see the Signor throw an egg several times nearly up to the ceiling of the vast theatre, and then catch it on a plate without so much as bruising it, or even making a sound. Later on, he breaks the egg before you to show there is no deception.

The Referee. "DRAMATIC AND MUSICAL GOSSIP."
January 17, 1886.

The world's most patient man is the American[71] Paul Cinquevalli, who dedicated nine years of his life to achieve the ability to throw a hen's egg high into the air and catch it on a plate, without it breaking.[72]

Hudiksvallsposten. "Ditt och datt." [Author's translation]
April 18, 1905.

To gain an authentic comprehension of Cinquevalli's juggling, one must fundamentally grasp that it did not revolve solely around the cyclical activity of throwing and catching more objects than hands available. This commonly held notion of juggling oversimplifies his approach.

When Cinquevalli explained juggling, he emphasized the integral role of balance,[73] as well as the art of catching a solitary object,[74] manipulating objects across various body parts,[75][76] executing feats like flipping a cigar from a balanced position on the nose into a holder in the mouth,[77] or launching a dart through a blowpipe to strike a turnip thrown high into the air.[78] While the continuous manipulation of multiple objects remained a component of his performance, it constituted only a fraction of the diverse array of object-handling activities encapsulated by the term "juggling." The pinnacle of his act resided in what he termed "The Human Billiard Table." To perform it, he would put on a green felt jacket, with pockets attached at the shoulders, hips and a fifth one at his lower back.[79]

"I will now play a 'game,' 50 up. Time me."

> The balls bounded into the air, rolled up and down the professor's body, in his ear (the sixth pocket), down his arm, round his neck, and along his back. They seemed never to stop for an instant. In the game of 50 he made only one slight mistake, and at the end of the five and a-half minutes the attendant who acted as marker shouted "Game!"
>
> *Otago Witness.* "A Chat With a Human Billiard Table."
> November 26, 1896.

The ending feat of the human billiard table act was an impossible balance:

> You would reckon it almost an impossibility, would you not, that one billiard ball could be balanced on another under the most favorable circumstances? Yet Cinquevalli not only succeeds in this, but does it on the butt of a billiard cue. Gradually this is raised till the point rests on another ball contained in a glass held in the mouth, and there it is balanced for some seconds.
>
> *The Sportsman.* "The 'World's Greatest Wonder.'"
> May 2, 1899.

Now I am a billiard table.

Otago Witness. "A Chat With a Human Billiard Table."
November 26, 1896.

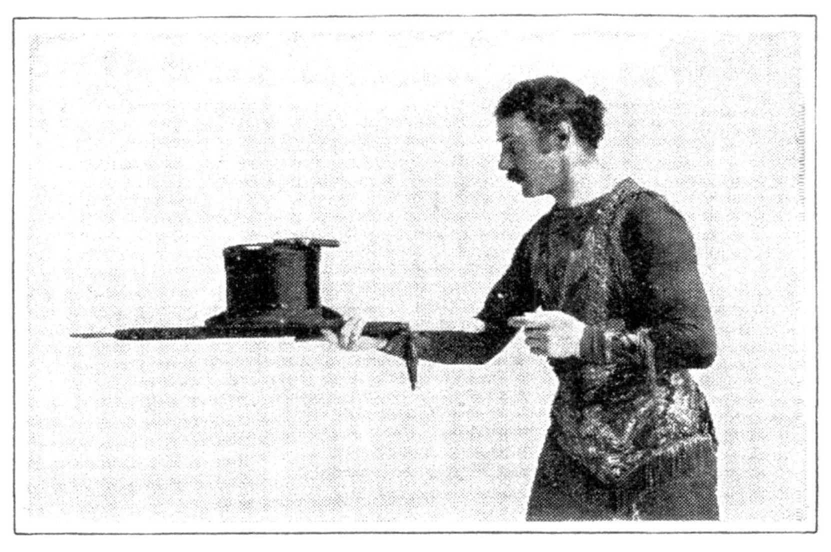

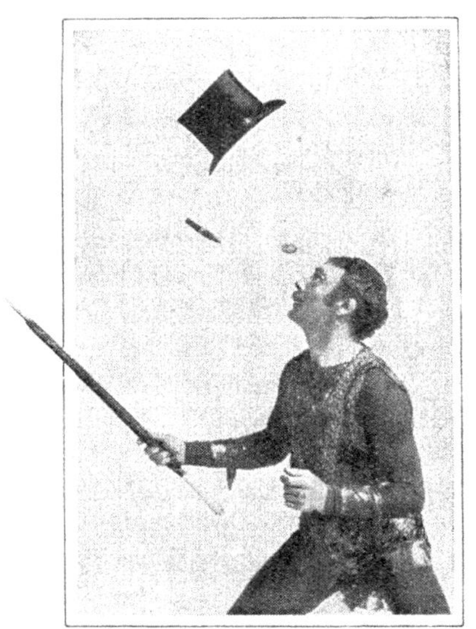

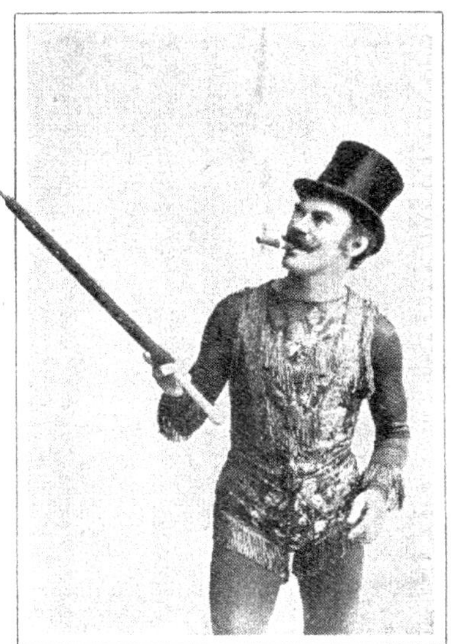

CLEVERER THAN GOD

It is all right, Mother; I can do it easily.

Cinquevalli, Paul. "JUGGLING TALES." *Sunday Magazine*, January 10, 1909.

Everything I appear to do, I do. There is no pretence.

Western Daily Press. "THE LAST TRICK."

July 17, 1918.

How is it possible?

How is it done?

Is he human?

The Sunday Press. "Entertainments. THEATRE
ROYAL. CINQUEVALLI." January 25, 1903.

By the way, I may state here that there is a great difference between juggling and conjuring. A conjurer makes you think he is doing things which he is really not doing. A juggler actually does what you see him do, and the feats he performs cannot therefore be said to be tricks.

Cinquevalli, Paul. "HOW TO SUCCEED AS A JUGGLER." *Cassell's Magazine*, March 1909.

What induced me to start? Well, I think I can only
say instinct.

The Bacchus Marsh Express. "THE KING OF
JUGGLERS." November 2, 1895.

Wonderful man is Paul Cinquevalli. Had he been planted down at the start in the Garden of Eden he would have set every apple on the centre tree going, in the air, at once, and used the snake as a necktie.

Gubbins, Nathaniel. "BRANDY AND SODA." *The Sporting Times*, July 11, 1896.

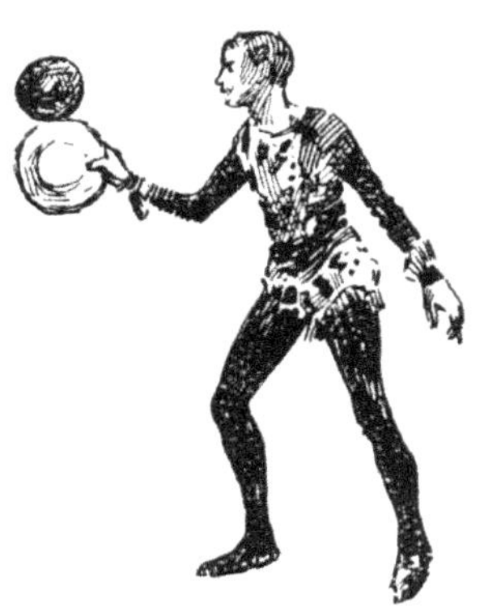

The man seems indeed to be a sort of Michelangelo or Leonardo of his profession. I am told that he can do in a general way – anything.

The Referee. "DRAMATIC AND MUSICAL GOSSIP." January 31, 1886.

Intended for the Russian Priesthood, Cinquevalli
Chose the Trapeze in Preference to the Church.

The San Francisco Call. "PAUL CINQUEVALLI
TELLS HOW HE ACQUIRED HIS
WONDERFUL SKILL." March 9, 1902.

If anyone had come on to do an "act" with a net for protection they would have hooted and shouted coward.

The Daily Mail. "AN ENGLISHMAN FROM CHOICE. CINQUEVALLI, THE JUGGLER, ON MANY THINGS." February 8, 1904.

I found the first trapeze bar clean and dry, and supposed the others were also. As I swung through the air at a terrific rate, fifty feet from the ground, I seized the second bar, but, to my horror, my hand slipped just as if the bar had been greased, and down I plunged headlong!

The Kansas City Star. "THE ART OF THE
JUGGLER." October 6, 1901.

NET! No, there was no net.

Gubbins, Nathaniel. "BRANDY AND SODA."
The Sporting Times, July 11, 1896.

I thought of my father and mother, thought of them as I had last seen them through the window seated by the fire in our cottage; I saw the fields, the school, the playground, and then pictured my parents as they attended my funeral. These and a hundred other things I thought of; then came a crash, and all was blank.

Chums. "EARLY DAYS OF A GREAT JUGGLER." November 13, 1895.

A broken breastbone, a broken leg, a fractured left arm, and a wrist reduced to pulp were a few of my injuries.

> *The Weekly Dispatch*. "PAUL CINQUEVALLI TELLS HOW HE BECAME THE TRICKIEST MAN ON EARTH." May 13, 1900.

~

For eight months I lay in bed only able to move one hand.

The Weekly Dispatch. "PAUL CINQUEVALLI
TELLS HOW HE BECAME THE TRICKIEST
MAN ON EARTH." May 13, 1900.

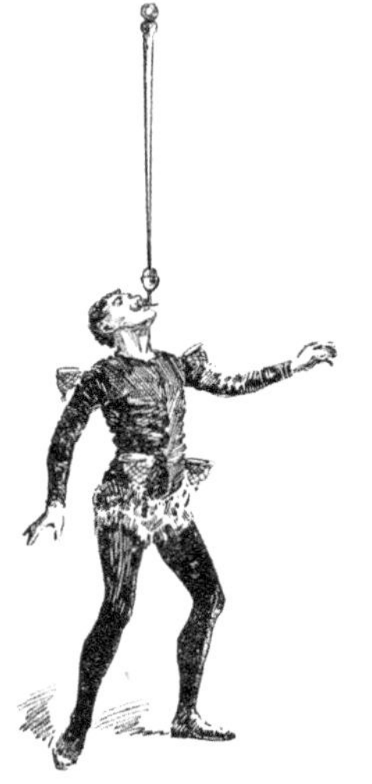

I think I broke every bone in my body; and I know I lay in hospital for a year and a half. And whilst there I made up my mind to one thing–that there should be no more flying trapeze for little Paul.

Gubbins, Nathaniel. "BRANDY AND SODA."
The Sporting Times, July 11, 1896.

The orchestra struck up a hymn of thanksgiving, and the whole of the vast mass of spectators knelt for a moment and crossed themselves. It had a tremendous effect upon me to think that they thanked God for my narrow escape from death.

The Showman. "Paul Cinquevalli." January 5, 1901.

He can speak either seven or seventeen languages –
I am not sure which – rather more fluently than his
native tongue, whatever that may be.

The Referee. "DRAMATIC AND MUSICAL
GOSSIP." January 31, 1886.

Is he cleverer than God, mother?

The Mail. "IS HE CLEVERER THAN GOD?
A NATURAL QUERY." October 12, 1914.

I often tell myself that I would give anything to be the equal of Cinquevalli, the juggler, or to be the captain of the largest Atlantic Liner.[80]

Bennett, Arnold. *Mental Efficiency and Other Hints to Men and Women*. New York: George H. Doran Company New York, 1911.

I will juggle in an original fashion...
or I will not juggle at all.

The Chicago Tribune. "THEATRICAL
NOVELTIES." February 22, 1889.

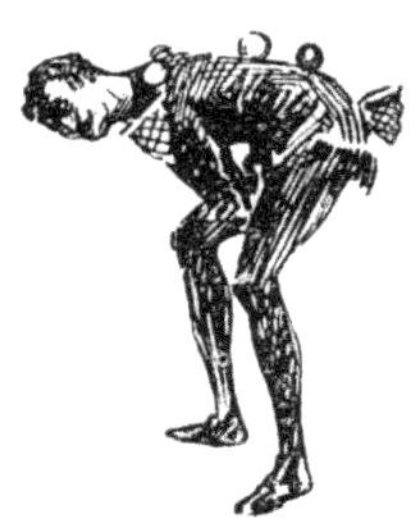

When I find that I have an imitator I invent something else.

The Pall Mall Gazette. "A GREAT JUGGLER
ON JUGGLING. An Interview with M. Paul
Cinquevalli." May 21, 1886.

His friends told him "You are a fool! What you are trying to do is impossible."

The Northern Star. "Wizard Feats in Jugglery."
October 29, 1910.

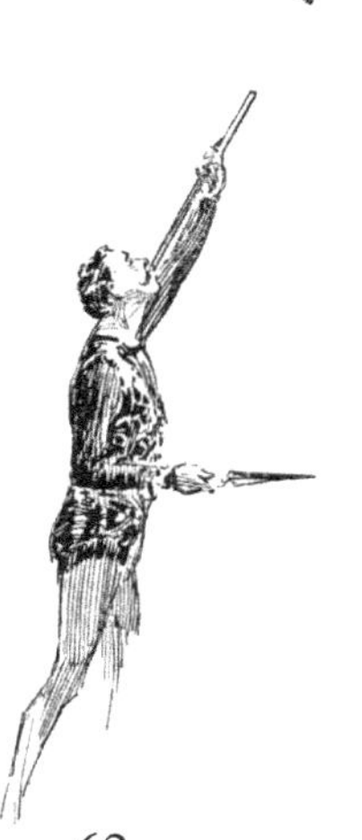

Tossing this globe of iron twenty feet into the air and catching it between the shoulders is a dangerous trick, for misplacing it a single inch either way means a dislocated shoulder, and a little higher up means broken neck.

The Kansas City Star. "THE ART OF THE
JUGGLER." October 6, 1901.

An error of judgement would, of course prove fatal; even to this day I feel goose-fleshy as the iron strikes me.

Stanyon's Magic. "MONS. PAUL CINQUEVALLI.
THE INCOMPARABLE JUGGLER."
January 1901.

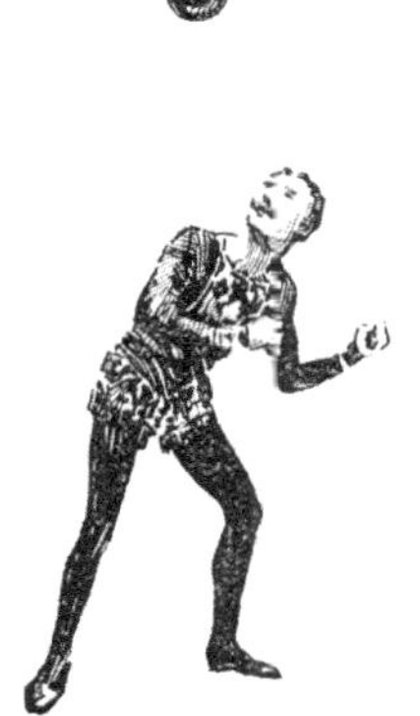

Let anyone try to catch that weight, in any form, in the same manner, and then ask him how he is.

The Poverty Bay Herald. "CINQUEVALLI. ONE OF THE WONDERS OF THE WORLD."
May 10, 1902.

CINQUEVALLI.
WILL CATCH THAT CANNON BALL,
FOR A THOUSAND YEARS, AND STILL
LIVE.
THAT IS WHAT HE SAYS.

The Herald. "CINQUEVALLI." June 19, 1899.

People are always telling me I will kill myself with
that ball. They are so kind.

The Critic. "Encore." February 24, 1904.

Paul Cinquevalli was knocked senseless by his cannon ball when appearing lately in London. He threw it up, as usual, with the confident expectation of catching it on the old safe spot between the shoulders, but owing to a slip of the foot, or a miscalculation in the throw, or in the placing of himself, poor Cinquevalli got the ball on his neck. He fell upon the stage as one dead, was taken to the nearest hospital, and is said to have remained unconscious for many hours.

The Wairarapa Daily Times. "MISHAP WITH A
CANNON BALL." February 20, 1904.

Cinquevalli is now in Belfast. He has given up dropping the cannon-ball on the back of his neck, just to please Madame Cinquevalli.

The Queenslander. "THE STAGE."

February 4, 1905.

It was reported a little time back that he had injured
himself while doing that risky trick with the cannon
ball, but he writes that rumour was a "lying jade."

Orpheus. "MIMES AND MUSIC." *The Evening
Post*, October 22, 1904.

Now some people think it impossible that I could receive that weight in my back. But some people also talk a lot about what they know nothing of.

Ireland's Saturday Night Journal. "THE WORLD'S
GREATEST JUGGLER. A CHAT WITH
CINQUEVALLI." June 4, 1898.

I have often been asked by young people how to go to work to be a juggler. There is only one way and one rule. It applies to any profession equally well, and that is: Whatever you make up your mind to do, stick to it until it is done. That is my system, and I have found it works very well.

The Examiner. "HAS HE A SIXTH SENSE?"
January 4, 1891.

It is fortunate—for Paul Cinquevalli, anyhow—
that he was not born three hundred years ago. He
would, without a doubt, have been hurried to the
stake as a being unmistakably in league with the evil
one.

The Entr'acte. "CINQUEVALLI RETURNS."
March 18, 1905.

You ask me about training? Don't drink, and smoke
as little as possible. It is difficult, but it is necessary.
The eye and the hand are delicate organs.

The Pall Mall Gazette. "A GREAT JUGGLER
ON JUGGLING. An Interview with
M. Paul Cinquevalli." May 21, 1886.

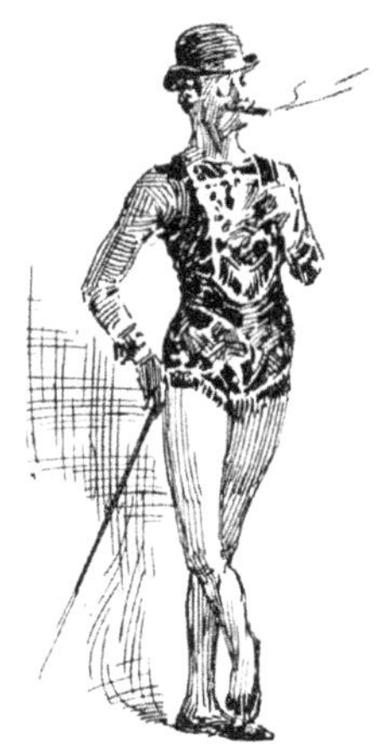

It has been said "see Rome and die," and while theatre goers are not advised to die, they can be recommended to witness the performance of Cinquevalli, who may be truly described as "the prince of jugglers."

The Ballarat Star. "THE CINQUEVALLI
SEASON - A SPLENDID PERFORMANCE."
December 18, 1902.

“Billiards,” said Mr. Cinquevalli, “is a delightful game which should be played in every home. There it can be enjoyed without the many temptations that assail the human man in saloons and places where he may be called to the bar.”

Cinquevalli, Paul. “HOW TO PLAY BILLIARDS.”
The Music Hall and Theatre Review, July 13, 1900.

I have in turn been convinced that Chartres Cathedral, certain Greek sculpture, Mozart's Don Juan, and the juggling of Paul Cinquevalli, was the finest thing in the world – not to mention the achievements of Shakespeare or Nijinsky.

Bennett, Arnold. *The Author's Craft*. George H. Doran Company New York, 1914.

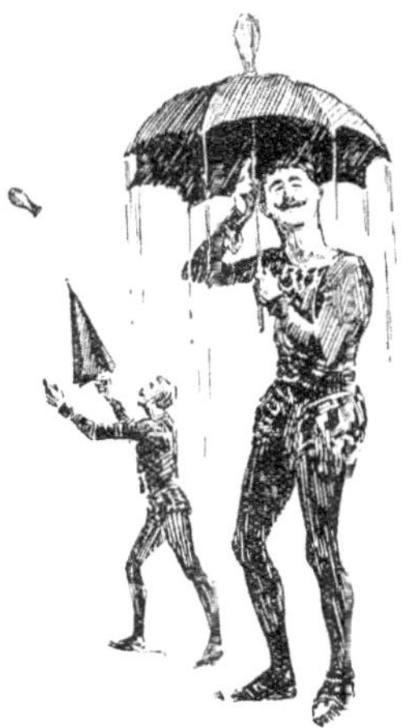

Twice already I have tried to retire from the profession. Once 16 years ago; once five years ago. It was no use. This body would not let me...

...I want to rest, and I cannot.
My body drives me on.

The Maitland Daily Mercury. "STORY OF A
GREAT JUGGLER." November 6, 1909.

Not yet, but some day, I shall notice my eye less quick, my hand less steady. I shall be compelled to retire. But if I cannot?

Stephens, A.G. "CINQUEVALLI'S BODY." The Auckland Star, July 3, 1909.

My nerves! They drag me back to the stage with irresistible power.

The Advertiser. "A GREAT JUGGLER."

August 7, 1909.

I may fail a hundred times but I keep on. And some
day I suddenly get the mastery.

The Maitland Daily Mercury. "A CELEBRATED
JUGGLER." August 2, 1904.

A friend bet me a champagne supper that I would
not do a trapeze performance from a balloon.
I took him.

The Australian Star. "ON JUGGLING. A GREAT
JUGGLER'S VIEWS." September 3, 1892.

He practiced one of his tricks for three years before he ventured it in public; another required five years of trial, and another eight.

Leslie's Weekly. "Cinquevalli, a Famous Juggler, and His Tricks." December 5, 1901.

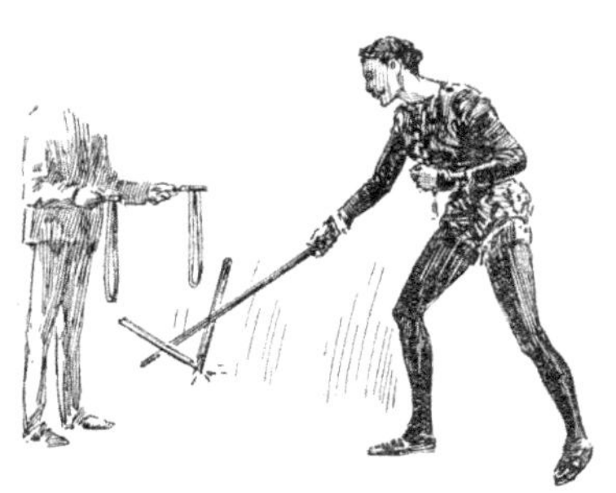

Cinquevalli, the greatest juggler living, whilst sitting at the piano can follow and play anything whistled by a person standing behind him, dictate a letter to his secretary, and listen to a conversation (which he will afterwards repeat) between other persons in the room.

The Bruce Herald. "NOTABLE PEOPLE."

July 3, 1900.

I never perform a trick in public until I am so perfect in it that there are a hundred chances to one against failure.

The Sunday Times. "TALKS WITH
THEATRICAL FAVOURITES." July 2, 1899.

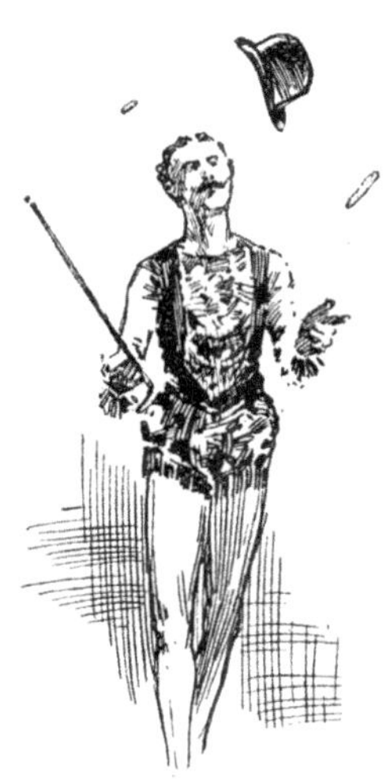

He holds the unique distinction of having appeared before the Prince of Wales twice in one day by command. On one occasion, when performing at Windsor, the Queen requested him to repeat several of his tricks two, and sometimes three times.

The Advertiser. "CINQUEVALLI. THE PRINCE
OF JUGGLERS." April 25, 1899.

The King of jugglers sets apart several hours of the day to practice every day of his life and will allow nothing to interfere with it.

The Wanganui Herald. "NEW ZEALAND AND AUSTRALIA." May 22, 1902.

First of all, I wish to impress upon you that juggling is not conjuring. There is no conjuring about my performance.
What I show to the public I actually do.

The Dalkeith Advertiser. "WITH THE WORLD'S GREATEST JUGGLER." August 1, 1895.

Practice every day? At least two hours without fail.

The Sketch. "A TALK WITH PAUL
CINQUEVALLI." December 27, 1893.

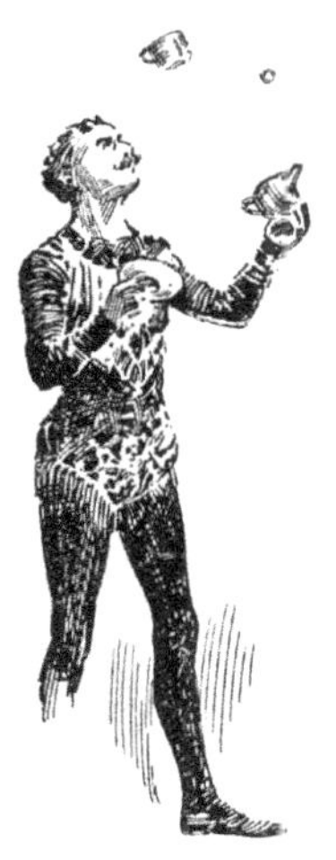

The hours and hours that M. Cinquevalli has spent in acquiring his simplest feat make an appalling aggregate. He practices literally till he is perfect, and for him to fail in public to accomplish a feat is unknown.

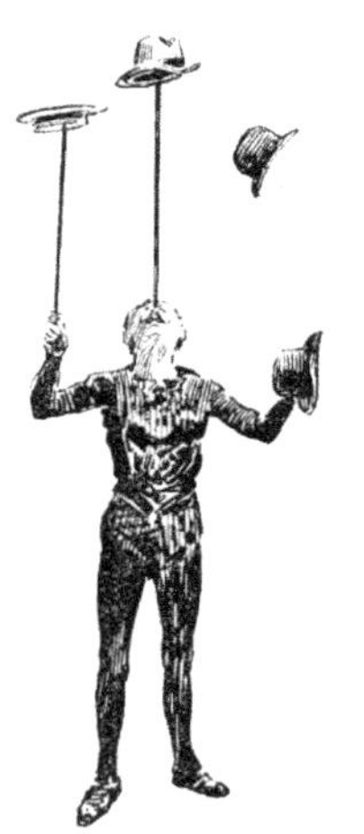

The Era. "PAUL CINQUEVALLI AT HOME."

March 11, 1893.

So absolutely has Cinquevalli got both his mental and physical powers under control that he can write a letter with one hand, keep two or three balls in the air with the other, and carry a conversation at the same time. He says it is all nonsense to think that people can only do one thing at once.

Pearson's Weekly. "WORKERS AND THEIR WORK." August 27, 1892.

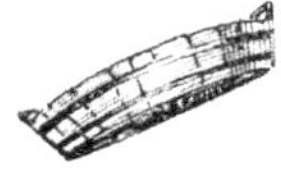

One feature that distinguishes the feats of the Prince of Jugglers from those of his inferiors is the fact that they are all absolutely original. He never attempts a trick that he has seen anyone else do, and if an imitator does manage to copy one of his own, he immediately drops it and invents another.

Pearson's Weekly. "WORKERS AND THEIR WORK." August 27, 1892.

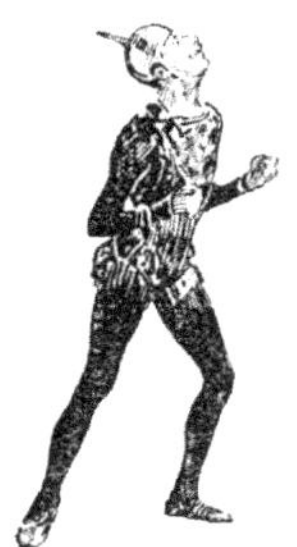

M. Cinquevalli is also a mesmerist. A sceptic came to him a few days ago. "Throw me into a trance," he said. "I defy you." "Look in my ring," replied monsieur, pointing to a large diamond on his little finger. Two minutes gone. A few passes, a concentrated look, the eyes closed, and the sceptic was under the influence.

The Pall Mall Gazette. "A GREAT JUGGLER ON
JUGGLING. An Interview with M. Paul
Cinquevalli." May 21, 1886.

This is the man whom the Prince of Wales commands to Marlborough-house for one trick every time His Royal Highness has a foreign visitor. When the Shah saw him there during his visit to England he was so much taken with his powers that he wished to place him in charge of the Persian Treasury.

The Argus. "PAUL CINQUEVALLI. A CHAT WITH THE FAMOUS JUGGLER." April 26, 1899.

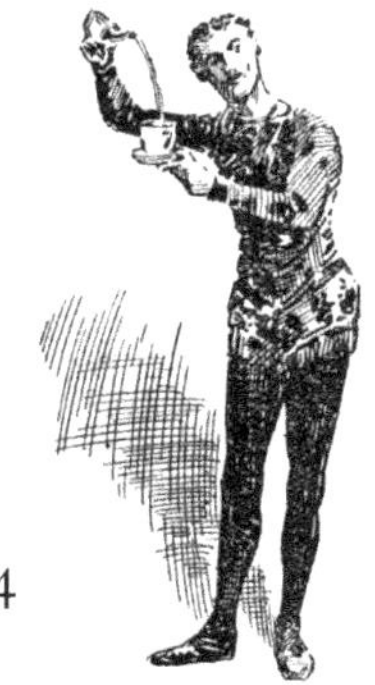

At the close of his performance he kissed the iron ball, his companion in many years' wanderings, before dropping it, with a resounding thud, upon the stage. The comedy was finished.

The Daily Standard. "CINQUEVALLI RETIRES."
November 21, 1914, Second edition.

I shall not be missed, only a name. Paul Cinquevalli, juggler — would that I could have made it more worthy of being remembered when I am gone. Nobody is any the better for having seen me. Others will take my place, and the crowds who today cheer me in the halls will pass me by in the street, without recognition.

The Daily Mail. "Death of Paul Cinquevalli."

July 17, 1918.

He was 59 when Father Time juggled him into oblivion.

The Australian Worker. "PARS ABOUT PEOPLE."
July 25, 1918.

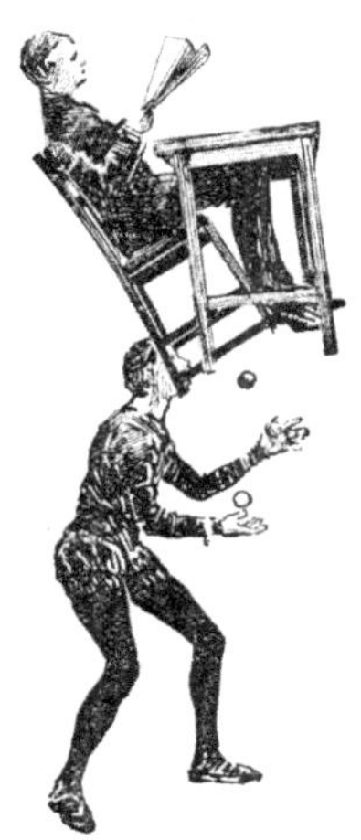

I do not know for what purpose we are here on earth; surely it cannot be that we should catch an egg on a plate. But there will never be another Cinquevalli.

The Londoner. Day in and Day Out. London, New York, Toronto & Melbourne: Cassell & Co. Ltd., 1924.

That was nothing.

The Pall Mall Gazette. "A GREAT JUGGLER ON
JUGGLING. An Interview with M. Paul
Cinquevalli." May 21, 1886.

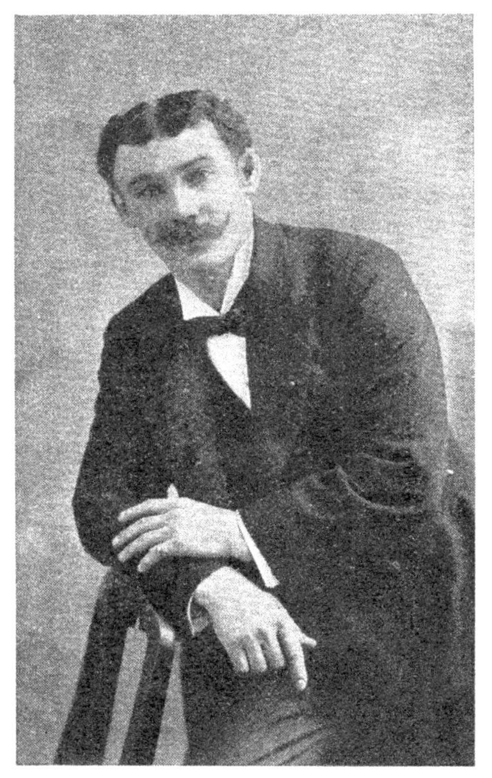

Sincerely Yours
Paul Cinquevalli

POSTSCRIPTUM

Having seen Cinquevalli you feel almost prepared to die, for there is no more jugglery left to live for.

The Bulletin. "SUNDRY SHOWS." May 6, 1899.

ABOUT THE
ILLUSTRATIONS

Photo on p. vi (6). Ca 1895. By Warwick Brookes. Author's collection.

Photos on p xxxvii (37). White, Stanley. "THE KING OF JUGGLERS." *Royal Magazine,* November 1901. Author's collection.

Photo on p. 100. By Warwick Brookes. Cinquevalli, Paul. "SLIPPING TO DEATH." *Wide World Magazine,* July 1904. Author's collection.

Signature on p. 100. Author's collection.

Monogram on p. 40. Paul Cinquevalli's letterhead, letter to Ellis [Stanyon]. 1901 January 15th. Mike Caveney collection.

Drawings on pages 40, 46, 54, 60, 62, 65, 74, 77, 83, 85, 89, 90, 92, 94, 97. *The Playgoer.* "PAUL CINQUEVALLI. The Greatest Juggler in the World." October 15, 1901. pp. 17-18. Charlie Holland collection.

END NOTES

1. The quote in its original form is from Joseph Addison's play *Cato* and is addressed to Sempronius. Oswald Stoll, the director of the Empire theatre appropriated the quote in his advertisements for variety performances.

2. George Alltree, who wrote *Footlight Memories* knew Cinquevalli well enough to be told trade secrets. See: *The Daily Advertiser.* "Cinquevalli's Secret." May 27, 1932. p. 3.

3. Henry George Hibbert who wrote *A Playgoer's Memories* knew Cinquevalli for at least 10 years, having been part of the inner circle at Adeline Cinquevalli's funeral. See: *The Music Hall and Theatre Review.* March 13, 1908. p. 173.

4. Lucas, Edward Verall. *A Little of Everything.* London: Methuen & Co., 1912. p. 27.

5. *The Graphic.* "Theatres." January 2, 1886. p. 7.

6. *Baily's Magazine of Sports and Pastimes.* "OUR VAN." February 1886. p. 259.

7. Braun Cinquevalli, Paul Emil Otto. "New South Wales Marriage Certificate." State of New South Wales, Australia, March 29, 1909.

8. *The London Gazette*. "The Naturalization Act 1870." April 4, 1893. p. 2083.

9. *The Mail*. "THE KING OF JUGGLERS - An Hour With Paul Cinquevalli." February 18, 1905. p. 7.

10. *La Exquella de la torratxa*. "Un cop d'ull als teatros." June 5, 1880. p. 5.

11. *Morgen-Post*. "Theater und Vergnügungen für heute:" June 4, 1879. p. 8.

12. *Neue Züricher-Zeitung*. "GRAND CIRQUE CORTY." July 28, 1877. p. 4.

13. *Berlinske politiske og Avertissements-Tidende*. "TIVOLI." September 27, 1878. p. 7.

14. *Lunds Weckoblad*. "Cirkus L. Houcké." October 5, 1878. p. 1.

15. *L'Intransigeant*. "PROGRAMME DU SAMEDI 18 FÉVRIER." February 19, 1882. p. 4.

16. Waller, Charles, and Gerald Taylor. *Magical Nights at the Theatre: A Chronicle*. 1st ed. Melbourne, Victoria, Australia: G. Taylor, 1980. p. 103.

17. Paul had been living in Paris for several years prior to his breakthrough in the UK, many might have assumed he was French, hence the French pronunciation of five.

18. Paul Cinquevalli was nicknamed "The Little Flying Devil" during his time as an aerial acrobat in Russia. See: *The Era*. "PAUL CINQUEVALLI AT HOME." March 11, 1893. p. 16.

19. Leszno, Poland in 2023.

20. *The London Gazette.* "The Naturalization Act 1870." April 4, 1893. p. 2083.

21. *The Sun.* "A FORTUNATE FALL. FROM ACROBAT TO JUGGLER." August 23, 1914. p. 14.

22. *The Era.* "THE LONDON MUSIC HALLS. PAUL CINQUEVALLI." February 20, 1886. p. 10.

23. *The Detroit Free Press.* "HOW TO BECOME AN EXPERT JUGGLER." February 19, 1902. p. 5.

24. It is also possible that his name was Stanislaus or Andreas, but that is a story for another time.

25. Leopold Cinquevalli, Paul's master.

26. *New York Clipper.* "PAUL CINQUEVALLI, PRINCE OF JUGGLERS." February 15, 1913. p. VIII.

27. *The Buffalo Express.* "CINQUEVALLI THE GREAT." February 7, 1902. p. 8.

28. *Evening Standard.* "NOTES ABOUT THE THEATRE." February 9, 1906. p. 5.

29. *Leslie's Weekly.* "Cinquevalli, a Famous Juggler, and His Tricks." December 5, 1901. p. 525.

30. *L'Orchestre.* "CIRQUE FERNANDO." September 11, 1881. p. 4.

31. *The Bulletin.* "At Poverty Point." June 24, 1899. p. 27.

32. *The Era.* "THE LONDON MUSIC HALLS. PAUL CINQUEVALLI." February 20, 1886. p. 10.

33. *The Era.* "PAUL CINQUEVALLI AT HOME." March 11, 1893. p. 16.

34. *The Sunday Times*. "Gossip About Theatricals." February 21, 1909. p. 18.

35. *Tit-Bits*. "A LESSON IN JUGGLING." June 2, 1888. p. 28.

36. *Paisley Daily Express*. "DRAMATIC CLIPPINGS." February 12, 1886. p. 3.

37. *The Illustrated Sporting and Dramatic News*. "Theatres." March 6, 1886. p. 634.

38. *Truth*. "Advertisement." April 15, 1886. p. 583.

39. *The Era*. "Notice." February 27, 1886. p. 10.

40. *The Illustrated Sporting and Dramatic News*. "OUR CAPTIOUS CRITIC. COVENT GARDEN CIRCUS." January 23, 1886. p. 472.

41. *Judy, or the London Serio-Comic Journal-*. "THE ONLY JONES." March 17, 1886. p. 124.

42. *Punch, or the London Charivari*. "EVENINGS FROM HOME." March 27, 1886. p. 149.

43. *The Entr'acte*. "MR. PAUL CINQUEVALLI. A PITCH-AND-TOSS CHAMPION." May 29, 1886. p. 9.

44. *Pall Mall Gazette*. "Acrobats at Practice." May 28, 1886. p. 4.

45. Codlin. "The Showman." *The Penny Illustrated Paper*., April 30, 1887. p. 285.

46. For instance, in the 1896 Christmas production of Aladdin, at Drury Lane, Cinquevalli plays the part of the Geni of the Lamp. See: *The Entr'acte*. "Merry-go-Round." January 30, 1897. p. 4.

47. 2nd USA tour, 1890: *Daily Alta California*. "AMUSEMENTS."
December 23, 1890. p.8.

48. 3rd USA tour, 1894-1895: *New York Times*. "Amusements."
December 22, 1894. p. 7.

49. 4th USA tour, 1896: *New York Times*. "NOTES OF THE STAGE."
January 7, 1896.

50. 5th USA tour, 1901: *The Liverpool Mercury*. "MOVEMENT OF
LIVERPOOL STEAMERS." September 5, 1901. p. 12.

51. 6th USA tour, 1905-1906: *Variety*. "CINQUEVALLI OPENS
MONDAY." December 23, 1905. p.5.

52. 7th USA tour, 1906: *The Brooklyn Citizen*. "DR. ZABRISKIE
RETURNS." October 3, 1906. p. 11.

53. 8th USA tour, 1907–1908: *The Chicago Sunday Tribune*.
"Vaudeville." October 13, 1907. p. 3.

54. 1st Australia tour, 1899: *The Age*. "AMUSEMENTS." May 1, 1899.
p. 6.

55. 2nd Australia tour, 1899: *Australian Star*. "STAGE, SONG, AND
SHOW." July 22, 1902. p. 3.

56. 3rd Australia tour, 1902: *The Daily News*. "AMUSEMENTS."
January 11, 1909. p. 3.

57. 4th Australia tour, 1909: *The Age*. "AMUSEMENTS." August 10,
1914. p. 5.

58. 1st South Africa tour, 1898: *The Music Hall and Theatre Review*.
"South African Notes." October 7, 1898.

59. 2nd South Africa tour, 1904: *Rand Daily Mail*. September 4, 1904.

60. An interview with a street juggler in 1861 claims there are no more than 20 jugglers in the entire U.K. Mayhew, Henry. *Street Juggler*. London, 1861.

61. Prior to Cinquevalli, the most successful performers of juggling, would mix in other genres of performing like magic or shadowgraphy in their acts. An example is Félicien Trewey, see: Colombon, Henri. *Treweyisme et Trewey*. Carpentras: Imprimerie Batailler, 1909.

62. *The Bulletin*. "SUNDRY SHOWS." March 1, 1902. p. 10.

63. H. G. "At the Red Mill." *The Bulletin*, November 3, 1904. p. 39.

64. See example D'Alvini: Burlingame, H.J. *Around the World with a Magician and a Juggler*. 1st ed. Chicago, Ill, USA: Clyde Publishing Co., 1891.

65. See example Karl Rappo: Ziethen, Karl-Heinz. *Juggling: The Past and Future*. Spijkenisse: Niels Duinker, 2017.

66. White, Stanley. "THE KING OF JUGGLERS." *Royal Magazine*, November 1901. pp. 383-387.

67. 10 stones roughly tranlsates to 63.5 kilograms or 140 pounds.

68. *The Bacchus Marsh Express*. "THE KING OF JUGGLERS." November 2, 1895.

69. *The Cambridge Independent Press*. "A JUGGLER WITH 3,000 TRICKS." August 13, 1909. p. 7.

70. *Sunday Sun*. "CINQUEVALLI - A Famous Juggler - His Confessions" December 29, 1907. p. 16.

71. The press was often confused about Cinquevalli's nationality, and sometimes he seemed to try and keep it that way.

72. Cinquevalli frequently "went viral" in the press, in the regard that the same article was reprinted in a plethora of newspapers, all over the world, sometimes translated. This article is an example of that phenomenon.

73. *The New York Dramatic Mirror*. "VAUDEVILLE STAGE. THE KING OF JUGGLERS." January 25, 1896.

74. *The Kansas City Star*. "THE ART OF THE JUGGLER." October 6, 1901.

75. Cinquevalli, Paul. "Twenty Years as a Juggler." *The Royal Magazine*. 1909.

76. *The Westminister Budget*. "A CHAT WITH A FAMOUS JUGGLER." November 24, 1893.

77. *The Picture Magazine*. "Pictures for Children. M. PAUL CINQUEVALLI." September 1894.

78. Fitzgerald, William G. "The Greatest Juggler in the World." *Strand Magazine*, January 1897.

79. Patent. Braun Cinquevalli, Paul. *Improvements relating to Dresses for Stage Purposes*. 6834. London, filed April 5, 1894, and issued May 12, 1894. Special thanks to Peter Brunning.

80. Spoken one year before the *Titanic* disaster.

51.433992 ° N, -0.099329 ° E

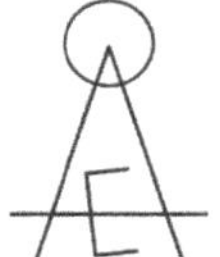

STOCKHOLM | **STOCKHOLMS**
UNIVERSITY | **KONSTNÄRLIGA**
OF THE ARTS | **HÖGSKOLA**